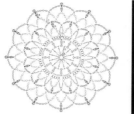

COMPLETE GUIDE
TO
SYMBOL CROCHET

by Rita Weiss and
Susan Lowman

Leisure Arts, Inc.

Little Rock, Arkansas

PRODUCED BY

PRODUCTION TEAM

Creative Directors:	Jean Leinhauser and Rita Weiss
Photographers:	James Jaeger and Carol Wilson Mansfield
Pattern Tester:	Susan Jeffers
Crochet Symbol Charts:	Susan Lowman
Book Design:	Linda Causee

Diagrams © 2013 by The Creative Partners™LLC
Reproduced by special permission

Special thanks to the International Marketing Division of Clover Needlecraft, Inc. for information they graciously supplied on the development of symbols in Japan.

PUBLISHED BY

LEISURE ARTS
the art of everyday living

© 2013 by Leisure Arts, Inc.

5701 Ranch Drive

Little Rock, AR 72223

www.leisurearts.com

Library of Congress Control Number: 2013910019
ISBN-13: 978-1-4647-1208-1

Introduction

This book was the idea of my friend and business partner, Jean Leinhauser.

Several years ago we had a project that required that we come up with over 400 different crochet stitches. Now, between us, we knew a lot of stitches—but 400? That's a lot! After ransacking every stitch guide either one of us owned, and even inventing a few stitches of our own, we realized that we had to dig deeper.

That started a great adventure!

Thanks to the Internet we were able to search just about every site that had crochet in Russian, French, Italian, German, Spanish and Japanese. No, we don't read all of those languages, but we can read international crochet symbols! And lucky for us those sites provided their instructions in crochet symbols. If we saw a sweater or a shawl or a jacket we liked, we could easily determine the stitch that was used!

And by the time the project was done, we had both learned a lot. First of all we probably needed better glasses. Those tiny symbols were often hard to read with our aging eyes! Second, the Japanese create the most innovative crochet stitches and use techniques we had never heard of before. And third—and probably most important—it is a lot easier to present stitch instructions with symbols than it is to write out the same instructions.

What Jean loved most about crochet symbols is that they look almost exactly like the actual stitches. You can look at a crochet symbol chart and work the piece right from that, with no words needed at all.

It was Jean's idea to be able to teach all crocheters how to read and use symbols. For a long time, very few of our American crocheters seemed interested in learning about symbol crochet. But then, we began to see many of our favorite crochet magazines including symbols along with their instructions.

Jean felt the time was ripe for her book, an encyclopedia of crochet symbols along with all the how-to necessary to turn our fellow crocheters into symbol crochet aficionados. Unfortunately Jean died before her work was finished; however, with the help of a loyal group of editors and designers, we have completed her project.

So come along and join us as we explore the wonderful world of symbol crochet!

—Rita Weiss

The Story of Symbol Crochet

Symbols for crochet instructions have been used for almost 100 years in most countries of the world except for the English speaking world where the choice has always been the printed word. Symbol Crochet is an international language composed of symbols, each of which represents and resembles a crochet stitch. If you know this language, you can work a design written for any audience, even if you can't say so much as "hello" in the language of the designer.

Japan has always been the country best known for the use of symbols; it may be the very country where symbols were first developed. The letters of the English language are actually based upon sound. The Japanese alphabet, which uses "Kanji" or Chinese characters, comes from drawings, and each character has its own meaning. For instance, the word for "rest" in Japanese is 休. The symbol for that word comes from the image that people rest near a tree.

This might be the reason why the Japanese preferred symbols rather than written patterns even in crocheting. Because they became used to this way of understanding, using symbols simplified the process allowing the crocheter to tell at a glance what each image means and to move forward.

Until 1955 publishing companies and crochet teachers used their own symbols. Many instructors and readers felt this was very inconvenient. In 1955 the Japanese Industrial Standards Committee (JISC) was called upon to establish some standards. This organization consists of many national committees and plays a role in the standardization of activities in Japan. It is their role to simplify and organize matters which are apt to become diversified, complicated and chaotic if left uncontrolled as was actually happening in the crochet world.

The first standards were established by that group on May 21, 1955 with a final revision made on November 1, 1995. Members of the group for both crochet and knitting include the Ministry of Economy, Trade, Industry, Education, Cultures, Sports, Science and Technology as well as the Japan Handicraft Instructors Association. Also an important part of the committee were publishers of handicrafts such as Nihon Vogue Company, Ltd, who were instrumental in codifying the symbols at the very beginning.

Today the JISC continues to be responsible for symbols and their use.

The Symbols

In symbol crochet each stitch is shown as a picture or a symbol that looks similar to the stitch itself. Shorter stitches are represented by shorter symbols while taller stitches are represented by taller symbols. These crochet symbols are sometimes grouped together, just as the stitches themselves can be grouped together.

⌒   represents a chain and looks like one.

● •   represents a slip stitch. It looks like a chain, but it has been filled in.

⊤   represents half double crochet

⊢   represents double crochet

⊧   represents triple (treble) crochet

Symbols can sometimes look slightly different from one publication to another. The slip stitch symbol can be made as a dot or a black oval; the single crochet symbol can be made as an "x" or a "+". The short lines in the middle of some of the other crochet symbols can be slanted or straight. In fact, all symbols may not be the same size; they can be slanted, elongated or distorted to fit better in a chart.

Symbols are often grouped together, just as the stitches themselves are grouped together for stitches such as bobbles, clusters, shells or popcorns (pages 41 through 47).

All of the basic symbols appear on pages 10 to 57. For help in locating a symbol, check the contents on pages 8 and 9.

The Diagrams

In order to make the work easy to do, the symbols are laid out in a chart into rows or rounds just like the crochet project itself. These charts are called a "Diagram." A diagram actually often looks like the finished piece, and will show how the piece is constructed.

Note: *Crochet charts are generally made for right-handed crocheters. Left-handers may want to copy a chart onto a transparency which can then be flipped over, turning the pattern into the best direction for left-handers.*

In projects worked in rows, such as the *Striped Scarf* on page 75, the first row is located at the bottom of the chart, and the last row at the top of the chart. Right side rows are read from right to left and wrong side rows are read from left to right if you are right-handed and the opposite if you are left-handed. Often—as here—charts worked in rows are drawn with alternating colors of symbols for each row, making it easier to follow each row in the chart.

In projects worked in rounds, such as the *Little Doily* on page 65, begin in the center of the chart and work around from right to left in a counter clockwise direction to the outer edge of the chart, if you are right handed, and from left to right (clockwise) if you are left-handed.

Two projects here, the *Granny Square* (on pages 60 to 64) and the *Little Doily* (on pages 65 to 69), will give you a chance to practice working a project from symbols. First we give you the complete diagram. Then on the next pages, we give you the symbols broken out in rounds in the left column and the pattern written out in words in the right column. Try working from the symbols, checking the work with the words.

As for these two projects, the complete symbol crochet chart is generally shown for small crochet projects. For large crochet projects, such as the *Pineapple Centerpiece* on page 88, it is common to only show a section or "slice" of the project in the symbol chart because of space limitations in the book or magazine. The chart will always show the beginning of the project, a full repeat and the beginning/end of the rows or rounds. The symbol chart will include the row or round numbers, located near the beginning of each row or round.

SYMBOL DIRECTORY

You have found a symbol, but don't know what it means?

Just look for that symbol on the next two pages. We give you the name of the symbol plus the page where you'll find illustrated instructions on how to create that stitch.

Contents

○	ch	10
● •	sl st	10
X +	sc	11
T	hdc	12
⟙	dc	13
⟙	tr	14
⟙	dtr	15
⟙	trtr	16
⌇ ⌇	FPsc	17
⌇ ⌇	BPsc	18
⌇	FPhdc	19
⌇	BPhdc	20
⌇	FPdc	21
⌇	BPdc	22
⌇	FPtr	23
⌇	BPtr	24
A ⋀ ⋀	sc2tog	25
⋀ ⋀ ⋀	sc3tog	26
⋀	hdc2tog	27
⋀	dc2tog	28
⋀	tr2tog	29
⋁ ⋁ ⋁	sc inc	30
⋁ ⋁ ⋁	sc inc	31
V	hdc inc	32

dc inc	33	
tr inc	34	
esc	35	
ehdc	36	
edc	37	
etr	38	
rev sc	39	
V-st	40	
3-hdc cl	41	
3-dc cl	42	
5-dc popcorn	43	
5-tr popcorn	44	

5-dc shell	45
2dc, ch 1, 2dc	46
3-dc shell	47
open picot	48
ch 3 picot	49
trP	50
picot with sc	52
crossed st	53
X-st	54
Y-st	56
adjustable ring	57

Chain
(ch)

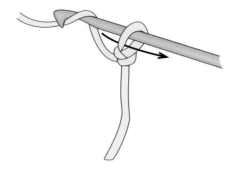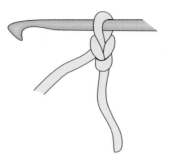

1. Bring yarn from back to front over hook and draw through loop on hook.

2. Completed chain (ch).

Slip Stitch
(slst)

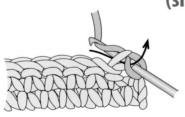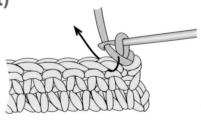

1. Insert hook in specified stitch, chain or loop.

2. Yarn over and draw hook through both stitch, chain or loop, and loop on hook in one motion.

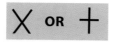

Single Crochet
(sc)

1. Insert hook from front to back in top of specified chain or stitch, and draw up a loop: 2 loops now on hook.

2. Yarn over and draw through both loops on hook.

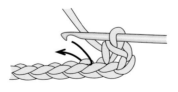

3. Completed single crochet (sc).

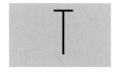

Half Double Crochet (hdc)

1. Yarn over, insert hook from front to back in specified chain or stitch.

2. Yarn over and draw up a loop: 3 loops now on hook.

3. Yarn over and draw through all 3 loops on hook; completed half double crochet (hdc).

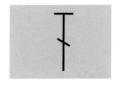

Double Crochet
(dc)

1. Yarn over; insert hook from front to back in specified chain or stitch.

2. Yarn over and draw up a loop: 3 loops now on hook.

3. Yarn over and draw through first 2 loops on hook: 2 loops remain on hook.

4. Yarn over again and draw through both loops on hook: completed double crochet (dc).

Triple (Treble) Crochet
(tr)

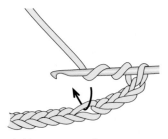

1. Yarn over twice .

2. Insert hook from front to back in top of specified chain or stitch and draw up a loop: 4 loops now on hook.

3. Yarn over and draw through first 2 loops on hook: 3 loops remain on hook.

4. Yarn over again and draw through next 2 loops on hook: 2 loops remain on hook.

5. Yarn over and draw through remaining 2 loops on hook.

6. Completed triple (treble) crochet, and one loop remains on hook.

Double Triple (Treble) Crochet (dtr)

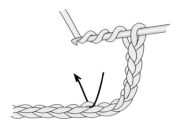

1. Yarn over 3 times; insert hook from front to back in specified chain or stitch and draw up a loop.

2. Five loops now on hook. Yarn over and draw through first two loops on hook.

3. Four loops now on hook. (Yarn over and draw through first two loops on hook) twice.

4. Two loops remain on hook. Yarn over and draw through remaining 2 loops on hook: completed dtr.

Triple Treble Crochet
(trtr)

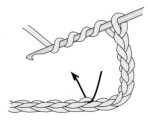

1. Yarn over 4 times; insert hook in specified chain or stitch and draw up a loop.

2. Six loops now on hook. Yarn over and draw through first 2 loops on hook.

3. Five loops remain on hook. (Yarn over and draw through next 2 loops on hook) 4 times.

4. Completed triple treble crochet (trtr).

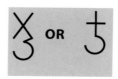

Front Post Single Crochet (FPsc)

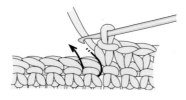

1. Insert hook from front to back to front around post (vertical bar) of specified stitch.

2. Yarn over and draw up a loop.

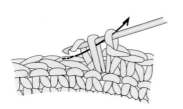

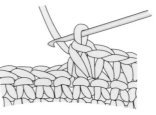

3. Yarn over and draw through both loops on hook.

4. Completed Front Post single crochet (FPsc).

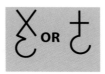

Back Post Single Crochet (BPsc)

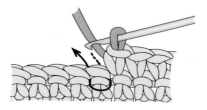

1. Insert hook from back to front to back around post (vertical bar) of specified stitch.

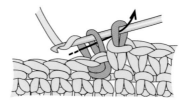

2. Yarn over and draw up a loop. Yarn over and draw through both loops on hook.

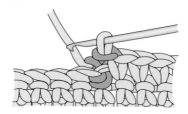

4. Completed Back Post single crochet (BPsc).

Front Post Half Double Crochet (FPhdc)

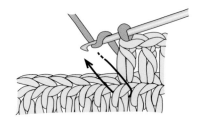

1. Yarn over, insert hook from front to back to front around post (vertical bar) of specified stitch and draw up a loop: 3 loops now on hook.

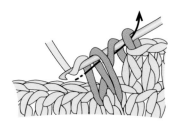

2. Yarn over and draw through all 3 loops on hook.

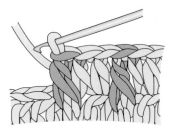

3. Completed Front Post half double crochet (FPhdc).

Back Post Half Double Crochet (BPhdc)

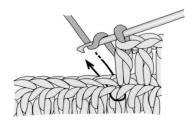

1. Yarn over, insert hook from back to front to back around post (vertical bar) of specified stitch and draw up a loop: 3 loops now on hook.

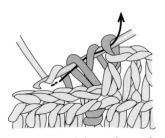

2. Yarn over and draw through all 3 loops on hook.

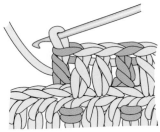

3. Completed Back Post half double crochet (BPhdc).

Front Post Double Crochet
(FPdc)

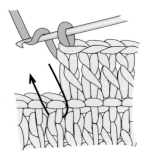 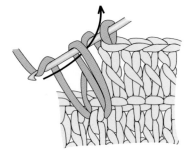

1. Yarn over, insert hook from front to back to front around post (vertical bar) of specified stitch and draw up a loop: 3 loops now on hook.

2. Yarn over and draw through first 2 loops on hook: 2 loops remain on hook.

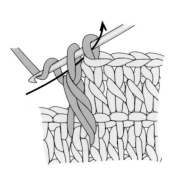 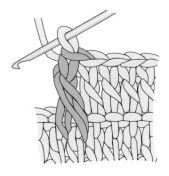

3. Yarn over and draw through both loops on hook.

4. Completed Front Post double crochet (FPdc).

Back Post Double Crochet (BPdc)

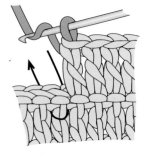 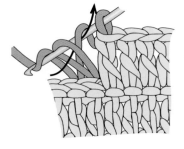

1. Yarn over, insert hook from back to front to back around post (vertical bar) of specified stitch and draw up a loop: 3 loops now on hook.

2. Yarn over and draw through first 2 loops on hook: 2 loops remain on hook.

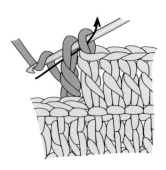 

3. Yarn over and draw through both loops on hook.

4. Completed Back Post double crochet (BPdc)

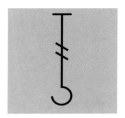

Front Post Triple (Treble) Crochet (FPtr)

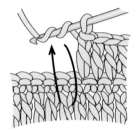

1. Yarn over twice, insert hook from front to back to front around post (vertical bar) of specified stitch and draw up a loop: 4 loops now on hook.

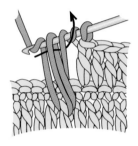

2. Yarn over and draw through first 2 loops on hook: 3 loops remain on hook.

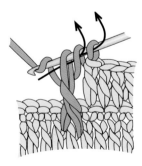

3. (Yarn over and draw through next 2 loops on hook) twice.

4. Completed Front Post triple (treble) crochet (FPtr).

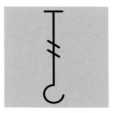

Back Post Triple (Treble) Crochet (BPtr)

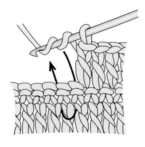

1. Yarn over twice, insert hook from back to front to back around post (vertical bar) of specified stitch and draw up a loop: 4 loops on hook.

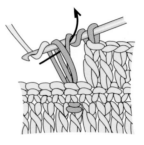

2. Yarn over and draw through first 2 loops on hook: 3 loops remain on hook.

3. (Yarn over and draw through next 2 loops on hook) twice.

4. Completed Back Post triple (treble) crochet (BPtr).

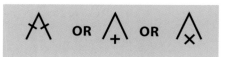

Single Crochet Decrease: Sc2Tog

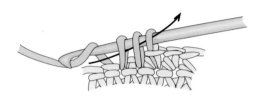

1. (Insert hook in next stitch and draw up a loop) twice: 3 loops now on hook. Yarn over and draw through all 3 loops on the hook.

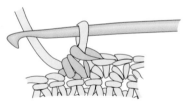

2. Completed single crochet decrease (sc2tog).

Single Crochet Decrease
(sc3tog)

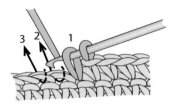

1. (Insert hook in next stitch and draw up a loop) 3 times: 4 loops now on hook.

2. Yarn over and draw through all 4 loops .

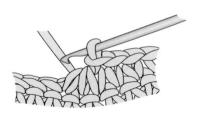

3. Completed single crochet decrease (sc3tog).

Half Double Crochet Decrease
(hdc2tog)

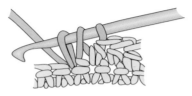

1. Yarn over, insert hook in next stitch and draw up a loop: 3 loops now on hook.

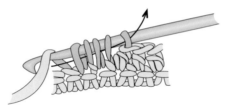

2. Keeping 3 loops on hook, yarn over and draw up a loop in next stitch: 5 loops now on hook; yarn over and draw through all 5 loops on hook.

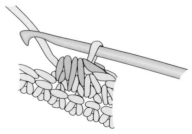

3. Completed half double crochet decrease (hdc2tog).

Double Crochet Decrease
(dc2tog)

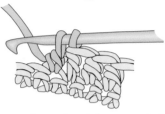

1. Yarn over, insert hook in next stitch and draw up a loop, yarn over and draw through first 2 loops on hook: 2 loops remain on hook.

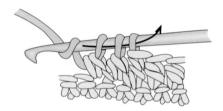

2. Keeping 2 loops on hook, work another double crochet in next stitch until 3 loops remain on hook; yarn over and draw through all 3 loops on hook.

3. Completed double crochet decrease (dc2tog).

Triple (Treble) Crochet Decrease (tr2tog)

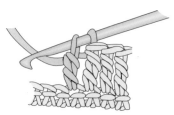

1. Yarn over twice, insert hook in next stitch and draw up a loop, (yarn over and draw through 2 loops on hook) twice: 2 loops remain on hook.

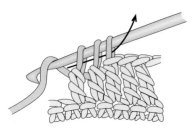

2. Keeping these 2 loops on hook, work another triple (treble) crochet in next stitch until 3 loops remain on hook; yarn over and draw through all 3 loops on hook.

3. Completed triple (treble) crochet decrease (tr2tog).

Single Crochet Increase: 2 Sts (sc inc)

Insert hook in specified stitch and draw up a loop, yarn over and draw through both loops on hook; insert hook in same stitch and draw up a loop, yarn over and draw through both loops on hook: completed single crochet increase (2 stitches worked into 1 stitch).

Single Crochet Increase: 3 Sts
(sc inc)

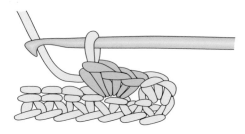

Insert hook in specified stitch and draw up a loop, yarn over and draw through both loops on hook; (insert hook in same stitch and draw up a loop, yarn over and draw through both loops on hook) 2 times: completed single crochet increase (3 stitches worked into 1 stitch).

Half Double Crochet Increase
(hdc inc)

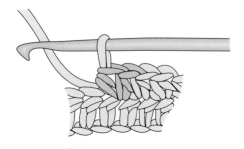

Yarn over, insert hook in specified stitch and draw up a loop, yarn over and draw through all 3 loops on hook; yarn over, insert hook in same stitch and draw up a loop, yarn over and draw through all 3 loops on hook: completed half double crochet increase (hdc inc).

Double Crochet Increase (dc inc)

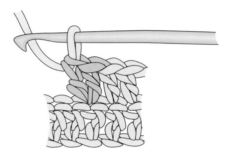

Yarn over, insert hook in specified stitch and draw up a loop, (yarn over and draw through 2 loops on hook) twice; yarn over, insert hook in same stitch and draw up a loop, (yarn over and draw through 2 loops on hook) twice: completed double crochet increase (dc inc).

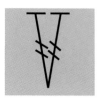

Triple (Treble) Crochet Increase (tr inc)

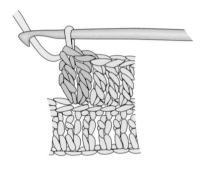

Yarn over twice, insert hook in specified stitch and draw up a loop, (yarn over and draw through 2 loops on hook) 3 times; yarn over twice, insert hook in same stitch and draw up a loop, (yarn over and draw through 2 loops on hook) 3 times: completed triple (treble) crochet increase (tr inc).

Extended Single Crochet
(esc)

1. Insert hook in specified chain or stitch and draw up a loop.

2. Yarn over and draw through one loop on hook.

3. Yarn over and draw through 2 loops on hook.

4. Completed extended single crochet (esc).

Extended Half Double Crochet
(ehdc)

1. Yarn over; insert hook in specified chain or stitch and draw up a loop: 3 loops now on hook.

2. Yarn over and draw through one loop on the hook.

3. Yarn over and draw through all 3 loops on the hook.

4. Completed extended half double crochet (ehdc).

Extended Double Crochet
(edc)

1. Yarn over; insert hook in specified chain or stitch and draw up a loop: 3 loops now on the hook.

2. Yarn over and draw through one loop on the hook.

3. (Yarn over and draw through next 2 loops on the hook) twice: 2 loops remain on the hook.

4. Completed extended double crochet: (edc).

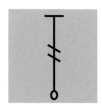

Extended Triple (Treble) Crochet (etr)

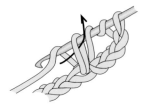

1. Yarn over twice; insert hook in specified chain or stitch and draw up a loop: 4 loops now on the hook.

2. Yarn over and draw through one loop on the hook: 4 loops remain on hook.

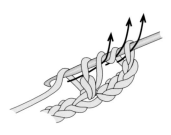

3. (Yarn over and draw through 2 loops on the hook) 3 times.

4. Completed extended triple (treble) crochet (etr).

Reverse Single Crochet
(rev sc)

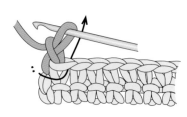

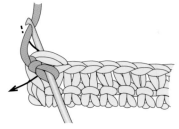

1. At end of row, do not turn, chain 1.

2. Working in opposite direction, insert hook in next stitch, to right (or to left if left-handed) and draw up a loop.

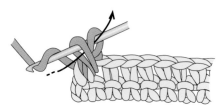

3. Yarn over and draw through both loops on hook.

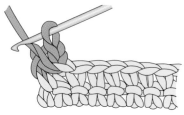

4. Completed reverse single crochet: (rev sc). Repeat Steps 2 and 3 for each additional reverse single crochet stitch across the row.

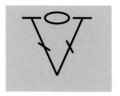

V-Stitch
(V-st)

(Two double crochet stitches separated by one or more chains, worked in the same stitch)

1. Work dc in specified chain or stitch, chain 1.

2. Work dc in same chain or stitch as first dc.

3. Skip one or more chains or stitches between V-stitches: completed V-st.

Half Double Crochet Cluster/Puff/Bobble (3-hdc cl)

1. Yarn over, insert hook in specified chain or stitch and draw up a loop: 3 loops now on hook.

2. (Yarn over, insert hook in same chain or stitch and draw up a loop) twice: 7 loops on hook.

3. Yarn over and draw through all loops on the hook.

4. Chain 1 to secure stitch: completed half double crochet cluster/Puff/ Bobble (3-hdc cl).

Double Crochet Cluster/Puff/Bobble (3-dc cl)

1. Yarn over; insert hook in specified chain or stitch and draw up a loop to height of a double crochet; yarn over and draw through first 2 loops on hook: 2 loops remain on hook.

2. (Yarn over, insert hook in same chain or stitch and draw up a loop to height of a double crochet, yarn over and draw through first 2 loops on hook) twice: 4 loops remain on hook.

3. Yarn over and draw through all 4 loops on hook.

4. Chain 1 to secure stitch: completed double crochet cluster (3-dc cl).

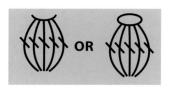

5-Double Crochet Popcorn
(5-dc popcorn)

1. Work 5 dc in specified stitch. Drop loop from hook. Insert hook from front to back under both loops of the first dc of the 5-dc group.

2. Insert hook in the dropped loop and draw dropped loop through the loop on the hook.

3. Ch 1 to lock top of the stitch in place: completed 5-dc popcorn.

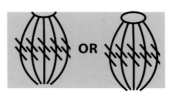

5-Triple (Treble) Popcorn
(5-tr popcorn)

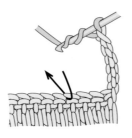

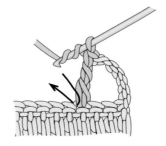

1. Work tr in specified stitch or space.

2. Work 4 more tr in specified stitch or space.

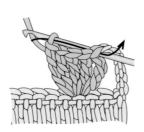

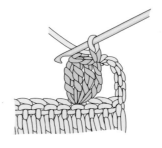

3. Drop loop from hook. Insert hook from front to back under both top loops of first tr of 5-tr group. Insert hook in dropped loop and draw dropped loop through loop on hook.

4. Ch 1 to lock top of stitch in place: completed 5-tr popcorn.

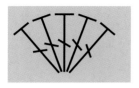

5-Double Crochet Shell
(5-dc shell)

1. Work sc in specified chain or stitch. *Skip 2 chains or stitches, then work 5 dc in next chain or stitch.

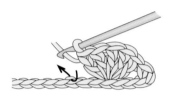

2. Skip next 2 chains or stitches, then sc in next chain or stitch: completed 5-dc Shell.

3. Repeat from * for pattern.

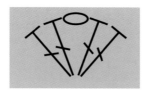

Shell
(2 dc, ch1, 2dc)

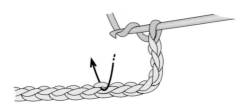

1. Work 2 double crochet in specified chain or stitch.

2. Chain 1.

3. Work 2 double crochet in same chain or stitch: completed shell (2dc, ch 1, 2dc).

3-Double Crochet Shell
(3-dc shell)

1. Work first dc in specified chain or stitch.

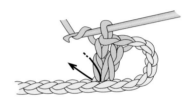

2. Work second dc in same chain or stitch.

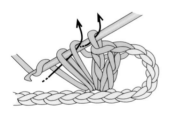

3. Work third dc in same chain or stitch.

4. Completed 3-dc shell.

Open Picot

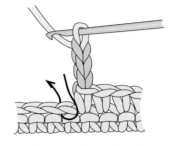

1. Work an sc; then chain 3.

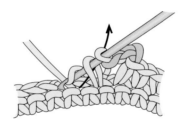

2. Insert hook in next stitch and draw up a loop; yarn over and draw through both loops on hook.

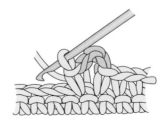

3. Completed open picot.

Ch 3 Picot

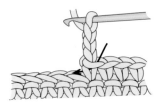

1. Ch 3, insert hook in front loop of base stitch and in left strand of same stitch.

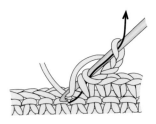

2. Yarn over and draw through all 3 loops on hook.

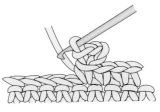

3. Completed ch 3 picot.

Triple Picot
(trP)

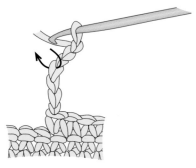

1. Chain 7, slip stitch in 4th chain from hook: first picot made.

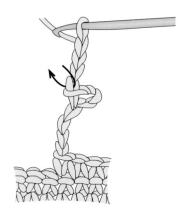

2. Chain 4, slip stitch in 4th chain from hook: second picot made.

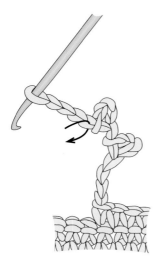

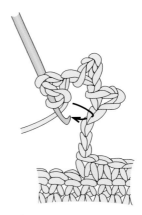

3. Chain 4, slip stitch in 4th chain from hook: third picot made.

4. Slip stitch in 4th chain of beginning chain-7.

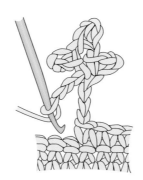

5. Chain 3: completed triple picot (trP).

Picot with Single Crochet
(picot with sc)

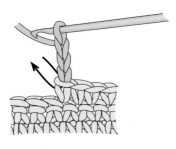

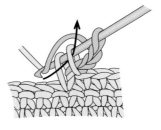

1. Ch 3, insert hook in front loop of base stitch and in left strand of same stitch.

2. Draw up a loop.

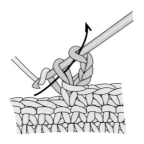

3. Yarn over and draw through both loops on hook.

4. Completed picot with sc.

Crossed Stitch
(CS)

1. Skip next stitch, dc in following stitch.

2. Working in front of last dc, yarn over, insert hook in skipped stitch and draw up a loop (3 loops now on hook).

3. (Yarn over and draw through 2 loops on hook) twice.

4. Completed crossed stitch (CS).

X-Stitch

1. Yarn over twice, insert hook in specified chain or stitch and draw up a loop: 4 loops now on hook.

2. Yarn over and draw through 2 loops on hook: 3 loops remain on the hook.

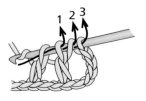

3. Skip the next 2 stitches. Yarn over, insert the hook in the next stitch and draw up a loop: 5 loops now on the hook. Yarn over and draw through first 2 loops on the hook: 4 loops remain on the hook.

4. (Yarn over and draw through 2 loops on the hook) 3 times: joined dc made.

5. Ch 2, yarn over, insert hook in top of joined dc and draw up a loop: 3 loops now on the hook.

6. (Yarn over and draw through 2 loops on the hook) 2 times.

7. Completed X-stitch.

Y-Stitch

1. Work tr in specified chain or stitch.

2. Chain 1, yarn over, insert hook in lower diagonal bar of tr and draw up a loop: 3 loops now on hook.

3. (YO and draw through 2 loops on hook) 2 times.

4. Completed Y-stitch.

Adjustable Ring

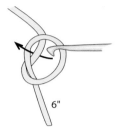

6"

1. Position yarn into a ring, leaving a loose end about 6" long. Insert hook in center of ring and under yarn coming from ball.

2. Yarn over and draw through: slip stitch made.

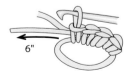

6"

3. Ch 1, work required number of sc (or other stitches) in ring. Draw on loose yarn end to close center.

Worked in Back Loop

The loop away from you at the top of a stitch. When working a stitch in a back loop (BL), insert the hook in the back loop only of the stitch instead of in both front and back loops, then work the stitch as usual. This symbol is placed below the symbol for the stitch in the symbol chart.

Worked in Front Loop

The loop closest to you at the top of a stitch. When working a stitch in a front loop (FL), insert the hook in the front loop only of the stitch instead of in both front and back loops, then work the stitch as usual. This symbol is placed below the symbol for the stitch in the symbol chart.

Join Here

This symbol shows you where to start the row or round.

Finish Off Here

This symbol shows you where to finish the row or round.

THE PROJECTS

If you'd like to try working a symbol pattern, here are several patterns as they might appear in a book, a magazine or online.

To help you, we've given you some hints on working the first two patterns: the "Granny Square" and the "Little Doily" on pages 60 and 65. At the left we have given you the symbols that tell you what to work for each round or row. At the right, you'll find the symbols written out in words. At first, try working from the symbols; then check your work against the words.

If you've never worked with symbols before, you might want to start with these first two patterns before attempting the more difficult ones especially the "Pineapple Centerpiece" on page 88.

Granny Square

Slightly different than the traditional granny square, but still just as satisfying to make! Our step-by-step symbol crochet charts will have you making this granny square successfully in no time!

SKILL LEVEL:

Easy

SIZE

5³/₄" (14.6 cm) square

GAUGE

Rnds 1 and 2 = 2 ³/₄"
(7 cm) square

MATERIALS

Worsted weight yarn
[100% acrylic, 6 ounces, 315
yards (170 grams, 288 meters)
per skein]
½ ounce red
½ ounce pink
½ ounce white

Note: *Photographed model made
with Caron® Simply Soft® #9762
Burgundy, #9719 Soft Pink and
#9701 White*

Size H (5 mm) crochet hook (or size
required for gauge)

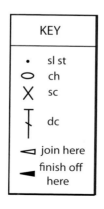

GRANNY SQUARE COMPLETED DIAGRAM

KEY	
•	sl st
○	ch
✕	sc
†	dc
◁	join here
◀	finish off here

THE SYMBOLS

Rnd 1 (right side):

Rnd 2:

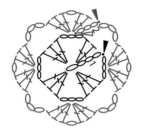

Rnd 3:

THE WORDS

Rnd 1 (right side): With white, ch 4, 2 dc in 4th ch from hook (3 skipped chs count as first dc), ch 3; (3 dc in same ch, ch 3) 3 times; join with sl st in 4th ch of beg ch-4: 4 groups of 3 dc and 4 ch-3 sps. Finish off white.

Rnd 2: With right side facing, join red with sl st in any ch-3 sp; ch 3 (counts as first dc), (2 dc, ch 1, 3 dc) in same ch-3 sp, ch 3; *(3 dc, ch 1, 3 dc) in next ch-3 sp, ch 3; rep from * 2 times more; join with sl st in top of beg ch-3: 8 groups of 3 dc, 4 corner ch-3 sps and 4 ch-1 sps. Finish off red.

Rnd 3: With right side facing, join pink with sl st in any corner ch-3 sp, ch 3 (counts as first dc), (2 dc, ch 3, 3 dc) in same ch-3 sp, ch 1, sc in next ch-1 sp, ch 1; *(3 dc, ch 3, 3 dc) in next ch-3 sp, ch 1, sc in next ch-1 sp, ch 1; rep from * 2 times more; join as before: 8 groups of 3 dc, 4 sc, 4 corner ch-3 sps and 8 ch-1 sps.

Rnd 4:

Rnd 4: Sl st in next 2 dc and in next ch-3 sp; ch 3 (counts as first dc), (2 dc, ch 3, 3 dc) in same ch-3 sp; *ch 2, skip next 2 dc, 3 dc in next dc, ch 2, skip next ch-1 sp, skip next sc, skip next ch-1 sp; 3 dc in next dc, ch 2, skip next 2 dc**, (3 dc, ch 3, 3 dc) in next ch-3 sp; rep from * around, ending last rep at **; 3 dc in top of beg ch-3, ch 2, skip next 2 dc; join: 16 groups of 3 dc, 4 corner ch-3 sps and 12 ch-2 sps. Finish off pink.

Rnd 5:

Rnd 5: With right side facing, join white with sl st in any corner ch-3 sp, ch 3 (counts as first dc), (2 dc, ch 3, 3 dc) in same ch-3 sp; *3 dc in each of next 3 ch-2 sps, (3 dc, ch 3, 3 dc) in next ch-3 sp; rep from * 2 times more; 3 dc in each of next 3 ch-2 sps; join: 20 groups of 3 dc and 4 corner ch-3 sps.

Rnd 6:

Rnd 6: Ch 1, sc in same ch as joining, sc in each dc around, working 3 sc in each corner ch-3 sp; join with sl st in first sc: 72 sc. Finish off white; weave in ends.

Little Doily

Learning to follow symbol crochet charts has never been easier. With our step-by-step charts, you'll have this pretty little doily done in no time!

SKILL LEVEL:

Easy

SIZE

6" (15.2 cm) diameter

GAUGE

Rnds 1 and 2 = 1¼" diameter (3.2 cm)

MATERIALS

Size 3 crochet thread
[100% mercerized cotton, 150 yards (137 meters) per ball]
1 ball yellow
Note: *Photographed model made with Aunt Lydia's® Fashion Crochet size 3 #423 Maize*
Size 0 (3.25mm) steel crochet hook (or size required for gauge)

 Instructions continued on page 66.

LITTLE DOILY COMPLETED DIAGRAM

STITCH GUIDE

Beg 3-dc cl (beginning 3 double crochet cluster): Ch 2, (YO, insert hook in specified ch-sp and draw up a lp, YO and draw through 2 lps on hook) twice, YO and draw through all 3 lps on hook: beg 3-dc cl made.

3-dc cl (3 double crochet cluster): (YO, insert hook in specified ch-sp and draw up a lp, YO and draw through 2 lps on hook) 3 times, YO and draw through all 4 lps on hook: 3-dc cl made.

Picot: Ch 3, sl st in top of last st made before ch-3: picot made.

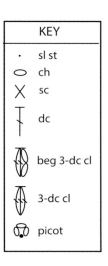

KEY	
·	sl st
⬯	ch
✕	sc
⊤	dc
beg 3-dc cl	
3-dc cl	
picot	

THE SYMBOLS	THE WORDS

Ring:

Ch 6, join with sl st to form a ring.

Rnd 1:

Rnd 1 (right side): Ch 1, 12 sc in ring; join with sl st in first sc: 12 sc.

Rnd 2:

Rnd 2: Ch 4 (counts as dc and ch-1 sp); *dc in next sc, ch 1; rep from * around; join with sl st in 3rd ch of beg ch-4: 12 dc and 12 ch-1 sps.

Rnd 3:

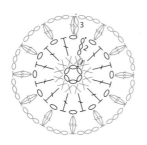

Rnd 3: Sl st in next ch-1 sp, work beg 3-dc cl in same ch-sp, ch 3; *3-dc cl in next ch-1 sp, ch 3; rep from * around; join with sl st in beg 3-dc cl: 12 3-dc clusters and 12 ch-3 sps.

Rnd 4:

Rnd 4: Sl st in next ch-3 sp, ch 1, 4 sc in same sp and in each rem ch-3 sp around; join with sl st in first sc: 48 sc.

Rnd 5:

Rnd 5: Ch 1, sc in same sc; *ch 5, sk next 2 sc, sc in next sc, ch 5, sc in next sc; rep from * 10 times more; ch 5, sk next 2 sc, sc in next sc, ch 5; join as before: 24 sc and 24 ch-5 sps.

Rnd 6:

Rnd 6: Sl st in first 2 chs of next ch-5 sp and in same sp, work beg 3-dc cl in same ch-sp, ch 3, sc in next ch-5 sp, ch 3; *3-dc cl in next ch-5 sp, ch 3, sc in next ch-5 sp, ch 3; rep from * 10 times more; join with sl st in beg 3-dc cl: 12 3-dc clusters, 12 sc and 24 ch-3 sps.

Rnd 7

Rnd 7: Sl st in first ch of next ch-3 sp, ch 1, sc in same sp; ch 5; *sc in next ch-3 sp, ch 5; rep from * around; join with sl st in first sc: 24 sc and 24 ch-5 sps.

Rnd 8

Rnd 8: Sl st in first 2 chs of next ch-5 sp and in same sp, work beg 3-dc cl in same sp, picot, ch 4, sc in next ch-5 sp, ch 4; *3-dc cluster in next ch-5 sp, picot, ch 4, sc in next ch-5 sp, ch 4; rep from * 10 times more; join with sl st in beg 3-dc cl: 12 3-dc cl, 12 sc and 24 ch-4 sps. Finish off; weave in ends.

Crossed Stitch Hat

Take your hat making skills to the next level with the addition of crossed stitches and post stitches for added texture.

SKILL LEVEL:

Easy

SIZE

Fits 19" to 22" (48.3 cm to 55.9 cm) head circumference

GAUGE

First 2 rnds = 3" (7.6cm)

6 dc = 2" (5cm)

MATERIALS

Bulky weight yarn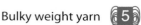
[75% acrylic, 25% wool, 3.5 ounces, 148 yards (100 grams, 136 meters) per skein]
1 skein blue
Note: *Photographed model made with Patons® Shetland Chunky #78108 Medium Blue.*
Size K (6.5mm) crochet hook (or size required for gauge)
Tapestry needle

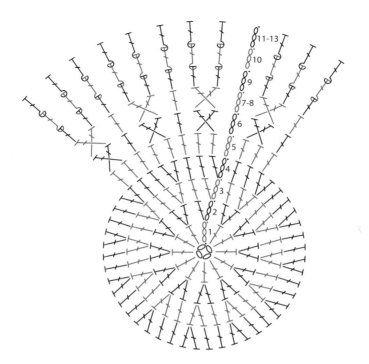

CROSSED STITCH HAT DIAGRAM

STITCH GUIDE

Crossed Stitch (CS): Skip next st, dc in next st, working in front of last dc made, dc in skipped st: crossed stitch made.

Front Post Double Crochet (FPdc): YO, insert hook from front to back to front around post of indicated st and draw up a lp, (YO and draw through 2 lps on hook) twice: FPdc made.

Back Post Double Crochet (BPdc): YO, insert hook from back to front to back around post of indicated st and draw up a lp, (YO and draw through 2 lps on hook) twice: BPdc made.

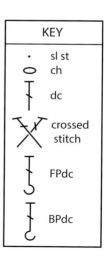

KEY	
•	sl st
○	ch
┬	dc
✕	crossed stitch
┰	FPdc
┰	BPdc

INSTRUCTIONS

Ch 4, join to form a ring.

Rnd 1 (right side): Ch 3 (counts as dc on this rnd and following rnds), 11 dc in ring; join with sl st in 3rd ch of beg ch-3: 12 dc.

Rnd 2: Ch 3, dc in same ch as joining, 2 dc in each dc around; join as before: 24 dc.

Rnd 3: Ch 3, dc in same ch as joining, dc in next dc; *2 dc in next dc, dc in next dc; rep from * around; join: 36 dc.

Rnd 4: Ch 3, dc in same ch as joining, dc in next 2 dc; *2 dc in next dc, dc in next 2 dc; rep from * around; join: 48 dc.

Rnd 5: Ch 3, dc in each dc around; join.

Rnd 6: Ch 3, work CS over next 2 dc; *dc in next dc, work CS over next 2 dc; rep from * around; join: 16 CS and 16 dc.

Rnds 7 and 8: Ch 3, work CS over next CS; *dc in next dc, work CS over next CS; rep from * around; join.

Rnd 9: Ch 3, dc in each dc around; join.

Rnd 10: Ch 3, FPdc around next dc; *BPdc around next dc, FPdc around next dc; rep from * around; join.

Rnds 11 through 13: Ch 3, FPdc around next FPdc; *BPdc around next BPdc, FPdc around next FPdc; rep from * around; join. At end of last rnd, finish off; weave in ends.

Snowflake Earrings

You'll love how quickly you can whip up a pair of these snowflake earrings. In just an hour or two, you'll have a finished project that you can proudly wear or give as a gift.

SKILL LEVEL:

Easy

SIZE

1¾" (4.4 cm) diameter

GAUGE

Rnds 1 and 2 = ½"
(1.3 cm)

MATERIALS

Size 20 crochet thread
[100% mercerized cotton,
400 yards (365 meters) per ball]
1 ball white
Note: *Photographed model
made with Aunt Lydia's® Fine
Crochet Thread #201 White*
Size 9 (1.4 mm) steel crochet hook
(or size required for gauge)
2 earring wires

     Instructions continued on page 74.

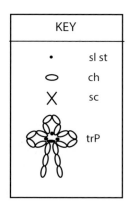

•	sl st
⬭	ch
✕	sc
	trP

SNOWFLAKE EARRINGS DIAGRAM

STITCH GUIDE

Triple Picot (trP): Ch 7, sl st in 4th ch from hook; (ch 4, sl st in 4th ch from hook) twice, sl st in 4th ch of beg ch-7, ch 3: trP made.

INSTRUCTIONS (MAKE 2)

Ch 5; join with sl st to form a ring.

Rnd 1 (right side): Ch 1, (sc in ring, ch 1) 6 times, join with sl st in beg sc: 6 ch-1 sps.

Rnd 2: Sl st in next ch-1 sp, ch 1, (sc, ch 1) twice in same ch-1 sp, (sc, ch 1) twice in each rem ch-1 sp around; join in beg sc: 12 ch-1 sps.

Rnd 3: Sl st in next ch-1 sp, ch 1, sc in same ch-1 sp, trP; *sc in next ch-1 sp, trP; rep from * around; join in beg sc: 12 trP. Finish off; weave in ends.

FINISHING

Starch if desired; attach center picot of any trP group to bottom of earring wire.

Striped Scarf

*Our scarf may look complicated, but it's really quite simple.
Once you understand the stitch pattern, you'll be off and running.
The use of 3 colors gives it that perfect look!*

SKILL LEVEL:

Easy

SIZE

7" x 55" (17.8 cm x
139.7 cm) before fringe

GAUGE

8 dc = 2" (5 cm)

6 rows = 2" (5 cm)

MATERIALS

Worsted weight yarn

[100% acrylic, 6 ounces, 315 yards
(170 grams, 288 meters) per skein

3 ounces red

3 ounces pink

3 ounces white

Note: *Photographed model made with
Caron® Simply Soft® #9762 Burgundy,
#9719 Soft Pink and #9701 White*

Size H (5 mm) crochet hook (or size
required for gauge)

 Instructions continued on page 76.

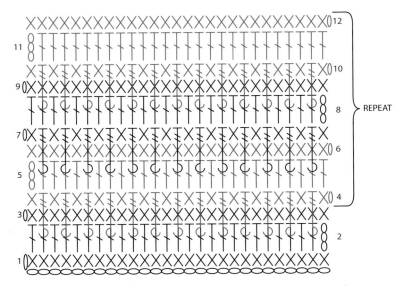

STRIPED SCARF DIAGRAM

STITCH GUIDE:

Front post tr (FPtr): YO twice, insert hook from front to back to front around post of specified st, YO and draw up a lp, (YO and draw through 2 lps on hook) 3 times: FPtr made.

Back post tr (BPtr): YO twice, insert hook from back to front to back around post of specified st, YO and draw up a lp, (YO and draw through 2 lps on hook) 3 times: BPtr made.

To change color: Work st until 2 lps rem on hook, drop first color, pick up new color and draw through both lps on hook, cut dropped color.

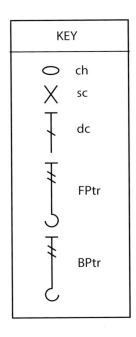

KEY
⬭ ch
✕ sc
† dc
‡ FPtr
‡⌐ BPtr

INSTRUCTIONS

With red, ch 28.

Row 1 (wrong side): Sc in 2nd ch from hook and in each ch across: 27 sc; ch 3 (counts as first dc of next row throughout pattern), turn.

Row 2 (right side): Dc in each st across: 27 dc; ch 1, turn.

Row 3: Sc in each dc across, sc in 3rd ch of turning ch-3, changing to pink: 27 sc; ch 1, turn.

Row 4: Sc in first sc, (*FPtr around post of dc 1 row below next st, skip next sc behind FPtr, sc in next sc*; BPtr around post of dc 1 row below next st, skip next sc behind BPtr, sc in next sc) 6 times; rep from * to * once: 7 FPtr, 6 BPtr and 14 sc; ch 3, turn.

Row 5: Rep Row 2.

Row 6: Rep Row 3, changing to white in last st.

Rows 7 through 9: Rep Rows 4 through 6, changing to red in last st on Row 9.

Rows 10 through 12: Rep Rows 4 through 6, changing to pink in last st on Row 12.Work Rows 4 through 12, fifteen times more. Finish off; weave in ends.

FRINGE

Following Fringe instructions on page 96, cut strands of each color 10" long. Knot 6 strands (2 strands of each color) in every other stitch on each short end of scarf. Trim fringe.

Sweet Sachet

What a great gift for Mother's Day or any day of the year. Fill this sachet with any scent desired, and use any color of crochet thread and ribbon to customize this sachet for any occasion.

SKILL LEVEL:

Easy

SIZE

4" (10 cm) diameter

GAUGE

Rnds 1and 2 =
1¼" (3.2 cm) diameter

MATERIALS

Size 10 crochet thread
  [100% mercerized cotton, 400 yards (365.76 meters) per ball]
  1 ball white
  Note: *Photographed model made with Aunt Lydia's® Classic Crochet Thread #1 White*
Size 7 (1.65 mm) steel crochet hook (or size required for gauge)
18" (45.7 cm) satin ribbon, ⅜" (1 cm) wide
Small amount fiberfill
Scented oil (optional)

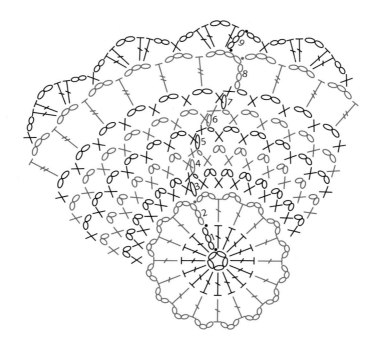

SWEET SACHET DIAGRAM

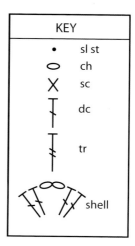

KEY	
•	sl st
⬭	ch
X	sc
⊤	dc
⊤	tr
〔shell〕	shell

Instructions

Top

Ch 5, join with sl st to form a ring.

Rnd 1 (right side): Ch 3 (counts as dc), 15 dc in ring; join with sl st in 3rd ch of beg ch-3: 16 dc.

Rnd 2: Ch 6 (counts as first dc and ch-3 sp); *dc in next dc, ch 3; rep from * around; join in 3rd ch of beg ch-6: 16 ch-3 sps.

Rnd 3: Ch 1, sc in same ch as joining, ch 2, sc in next ch-3 sp; *ch 2, sc in next dc, ch 2, sc in next ch-3 sp; rep from * around; join with ch 1, sc in beg sc (counts as last ch-2 sp): 32 ch-2 sps.

Rnds 4 through 7: Ch 1, sc in last ch-2 sp made on previous rnd; *ch 2, sc in next ch-2 sp; rep from * around; join with ch 1, sc in beg sc.

Rnd 8: Ch 7 (counts as tr and ch-3 sp); *tr in next ch-2 sp, ch 3; rep from * around; join with sl st in 4th ch of beg ch-7: 32 ch-3 sps.

Rnd 9: Sl st in next ch-3 sp, ch 3 (counts as dc), (dc, ch 2, 2 dc) in same ch-3 sp (beg shell made), ch 2, sc in next ch-3 sp, ch 2; *shell in next ch-3 sp, ch 2, sc in next ch-3 sp, ch 2; rep from * around; join in 3rd ch of beg ch-3: 16 shells. Finish off; weave in ends.

Bottom

Work same as top.

Finishing

If desired, apply scented oil to fiberfill, set aside. Hold Top and Bottom with wrong sides together; weave ribbon through Rnd 8 on both pieces; insert scented fiberfill before closing. Tie ribbon in a bow.

Kitchen Angel Dishcloth

With this beautiful angel washcloth, you'll actually want to do your dishes!!! Complete with halo and wings, she'll add a touch of elegance to any kitchen.

SKILL LEVEL:

Easy ◼◼◻◻

SIZE

4½" (11.4 cm) tall without halo

GAUGE

11 dc = 2" (5 cm)

MATERIALS

Light worsted weight yarn

[100% mercerized cotton, 3.5 ounces, 218 yards (100 grams, 199 meters) per skein]

1 ball white

30 yds blue

Note: *Photographed model made with Omega Sinfonia #801 White and #865 Blue Orchid*

Size D (3.25mm) crochet hook (or size required for gauge)

Stitch marker

 Instructions continued on page 82.

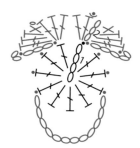

Head, Wings & Halo
Rnds 1-2

STITCH GUIDE

Post: Vertical bar of any st. To work a post st, insert hook from front to back to front around post of specified st, complete as indicated in pattern.

Note: *To join with sc, make a slip knot and place on hook, insert hook in indicated st and draw up a lp, YO and draw through both lps on hook.*

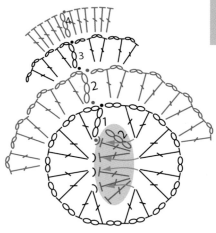

Skirt Rnds 1-4

KEY	
•	sl st
◯	ch
✕	sc
⊤	dc
⌣	front lp
◁	join here
◀	finish off here

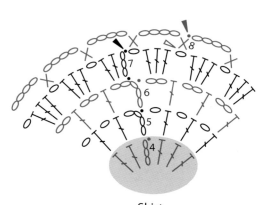

Skirt
Rnds 5-8

INSTRUCTIONS

HEAD

With white, ch 4 (counts as first dc).

Rnd 1: Work 10 dc in 4th ch from hook; join with sl st in 4th ch of beg ch-4: 11 dc.

WINGS AND HALO

Rnd 2: Ch 3 (mark ch-3 sp for st placement later), 2 dc in same ch as joining, 3 dc in next dc, ch 1; work (sc, hdc, dc, tr) around post of last dc made; ch 2, sl st in top of last tr made, ch 3, sl st around same dc post as previous sts, sl st in next 3 dc on head; ch 12 for halo, skip next 3 sts on head, sl st in next 3 sts on head and in marked ch-3 sp, ch 5, sl st in 3rd ch from hook; work (tr, dc, hdc, sc) in same marked ch-3 sp; join in FLO of next dc on wings. (**Note:** *This dc may be hidden somewhat under previous sts. Push wing back so as not to skip st*).

SKIRT

Rnd 1: Ch 5 (counts as first dc and ch-2 sp), dc in FLO of same st as joining, ch 2; (dc, ch 2) twice in FLO of each of next 3 sts, turn; working in front of sts just made and into free lps of same 4 sts on wings, work (dc, ch 2) twice in each of next 4 dc; join in 3rd ch of beg ch-5: 16 dc and 16 ch-2 sps.

Rnd 2: Sl st in next ch-2 sp, ch 5, dc in same ch-2 sp, ch 2; *(dc, ch 2) twice in next ch-2 sp; rep from * around; join in 3rd ch of beg ch-5: 32 dc and 32 ch-2 sps.

Rnd 3: Rep Rnd 2: 64 dc and 64 ch-2 sps.

Rnd 4: Ch 3 (counts as dc), 2 dc in next ch-2 sp; *dc in next dc, 2 dc in next ch-2 sp; rep from * around; join in top of beg ch-3: 192 dc.

Rnd 5: Ch 4 (counts as dc and ch-1 sp); *dc in next dc, ch 1; rep from * around; join in 3rd ch of beg ch-4.

Rnd 6: Ch 5; *dc in next dc, ch 2; rep from * around; join in 3rd ch of beg ch-5.

Rnd 7: Sl st in next ch-2 sp, ch 3, 2 dc in same ch-2 sp, ch 1; *3 dc in next ch-2 sp, ch 1; rep from * around; join in top of beg ch-3. Finish off.

Rnd 8: Join blue with sc in any ch-1 sp, ch 4; *sc in next ch-1 sp, ch 4; rep from * around; join in beg sc. Finish off; weave in ends.

Galaxy Doily

Made with 2 colors, this doily has charm! And it's easy to make with the addition of our symbol crochet chart.

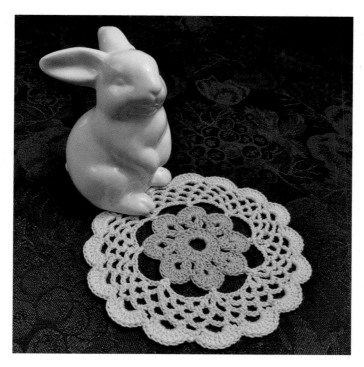

SKILL LEVEL:

Easy

SIZE

4¾" (12.1 cm) diameter

GAUGE

Rnds 1 through 3 = 2" (5 cm) diameter

MATERIALS

Size 10 crochet thread
[100% mercerized cotton, 350 yards (274.32 meters) per ball]
1 ball green
1 ball natural

Note: *Photographed model made with Aunt Lydia's® Classic Crochet Thread #661 Frosty Green and #226 Natural.*

Size 7 (1.65mm) steel crochet hook (or size required for gauge)

 Instructions continued on page 86.

DIAGRAM FOR GALAXY DOILY

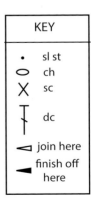

KEY	
•	sl st
O	ch
X	sc
T	dc
◁	join here
◀	finish off here

INSTRUCTIONS

With green, ch 10, join with sl st to form a ring.

Rnd 1 (right side): Ch 3 (counts as dc here and throughout), 23 dc in ring; join with sl st in 3rd ch of beg ch-3: 24 dc.

Rnd 2: Ch 3, (dc, ch 3, 2 dc) in same ch as joining; *ch 1, skip next 2 dc, (2 dc, ch 3, 2 dc) in next dc; rep from * around; join with sc in 3rd ch of beg ch-3 (counts as last ch-1 sp): 32 dc, 8 ch-3 sps and 8 ch-1 sps.

Rnd 3: Ch 1, sc around post of joining sc, 9 dc in next ch-3 sp; *sc in next ch-1 sp, 9 dc in next ch-3 sp; rep from * around; join with sl st in first sc: 8 groups of 9 dc and 8 sc. Finish off.

Rnd 4: With right side facing, join natural with sc in center dc of any 9-dc group, ch 11; *sc in center dc of next 9-dc group, ch 11; rep from * around; join with sl st in first sc: 8 ch-11 sps and 8 sc.

Rnd 5: Ch 1, sc in same sc as joining; *(ch 4, sk next 2 chs, sc in next ch) 3 times, ch 4, sk next 2 chs**, sc in next sc; rep from * around, ending last rep at **; join as before: 32 sc and 32 ch-4 sps.

Rnds 6 through 8: Sl st in first 2 chs of next ch-4 sp, ch 1, sc in same ch-4 sp, ch 4; *sc in next ch-4 sp, ch 4; rep from * around; join.

Rnd 9: Sl st in first 2 chs of next ch-4 sp, ch 1, sc in same ch-4 sp, 9 dc in next ch-4 sp; *sc in next ch-4 sp, 9 dc in next ch-4 sp; rep from * around; join: 16 groups of 9 dc and 16 sc. Finish off; weave in ends.

FINISHING

Wash and block.

Pineapple Centerpiece

If you love the look of crocheted pineapples, give this centerpiece a try! With the addition of our symbol crochet charts, you'll be able to visually see where to start and stop each point of the pineapples.

SKILL LEVEL:

Intermediate

SIZE

13" (33 cm) diameter

GAUGE

Rnds 1 through 3 =
2" (5 cm) diameter

MATERIALS

Size 10 crochet thread

[100% mercerized cotton, 350 yards (274.32 meters) per ball

1 ball natural

Note: *Photographed model made with Aunt Lydia's® Classic Crochet Thread #226 Natural.*

Size 7 (1.65 mm) steel crochet hook (or size required for gauge)

DIAGRAM FOR PINEAPPLE CENTERPIECE

Stitch Guide

Beginning shell (beg shell): Ch 3, (dc, ch 2, 2 dc) in specified st or sp: beg shell made.

Shell: Work (2 dc, ch 2, 2 dc) in specified st or sp: shell made.

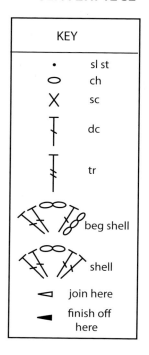

KEY	
•	sl st
○	ch
X	sc
⊤	dc
⊤	tr
	beg shell
	shell
◁	join here
◀	finish off here

Instructions continued on page 90

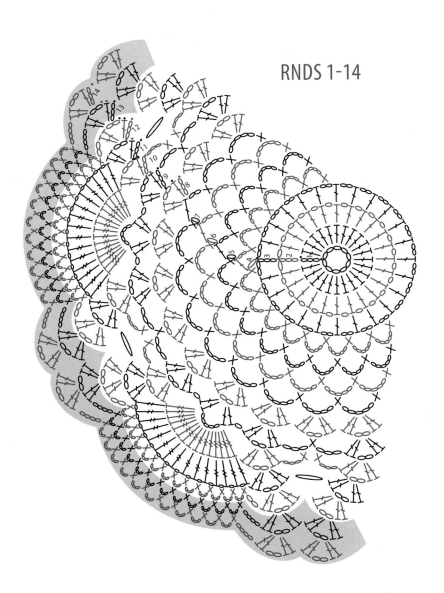

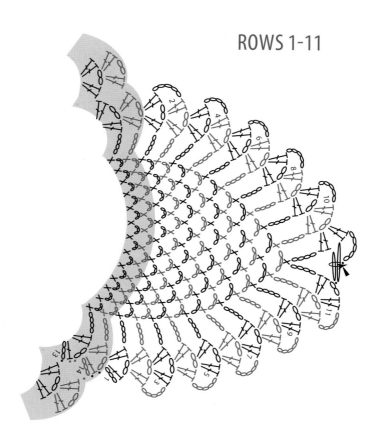

Instructions

Ch 10, join with sl st to form a ring.

Rnd 1 (right side): Ch 3 (counts as dc here and throughout), 23 dc in ring; join with sl st in 3rd ch of beg ch-3: 24 dc.

Rnd 2: Ch 4 (counts as dc and ch-1 sp); *dc in next dc, ch 1; rep from * around; join with sl st in 3rd ch of beg ch-4: 24 dc and 24 ch-1 sps.

Rnd 3: Ch 5 (counts as dc and ch-2 sp); *dc in next dc, ch 2; rep from * around; join with sl st in 3rd ch of beg ch-5: 24 dc and 24 ch-2 sps.

Rnd 4: Ch 1, sc in next ch-2 sp; *ch 5, sc in next ch-2 sp; rep from * around; join with ch 2, dc in first sc (counts as last ch-5 sp): 24 ch-5 sps and 24 sc.

Rnds 5 through 7: Ch 1, sc around post of joining dc; *ch 5, sc in next ch-5 sp; rep from * around; join as before.

Rnd 8: Work beg shell in first ch-5 sp (around post of joining dc), shell in next ch-5 sp and in each ch-5 sp around; join in 3rd ch of beg ch-3: 24 shells.

Rnd 9: Sl st in next dc and in ch-sp of next shell, work beg shell in same ch-sp; *ch 1, (2 dc, ch 5, 2 dc) in ch-sp of next shell, ch 1, shell in ch-sp of next shell, ch 3, sc in ch-sp of next shell, ch 3**, shell in ch-sp of next shell; rep from * around, ending last rep at **; join as before: 12 shells, 6 ch-5 sps, and 6 sc.

Rnd 10: Sl st in next dc and in ch-sp of next shell, work beg shell in same ch-sp; *15 tr in next ch-5 sp, shell in ch-sp of next shell, ch 3, sc in each of next 2 ch-3 sps, ch 3**, shell in ch-sp of next shell; rep from * around, ending last rep at **; join: 12 shells, 6 groups of 15 tr and 12 sc.

Rnd 11: Sl st in next dc and in ch-sp of next shell, work beg shell in same ch-sp; *(tr in next tr, ch 1) 14 times, tr in next tr, shell in ch-sp of next shell, ch 1, skip next 2 sc**, shell in ch-sp of next shell; rep from * around, ending last rep at **; join: 12 shells, 90 tr and 90 ch-1 sps.

Rnd 12: Sl st in next dc and in ch-sp of next shell, work beg shell in same ch-sp; *ch 2, sc in next ch-1 sp, (ch 3, sc in next ch-1 sp) 13 times, ch 2, shell in ch-sp of next shell**, shell in ch-sp of next shell; rep from * around, ending last rep at **; join: 12 shells, 78 ch-3 sps and 12 ch-2 sps.

Rnd 13: Sl st in next dc and in ch-sp of next shell, work beg shell in same ch-sp; *ch 4, sc in next ch-3 sp, (ch 3, sc in next ch-3 sp) 12 times, ch 4, shell in ch-sp of next shell**, shell in ch-sp of next shell; rep from * around, ending last rep at **; join: 12 shells, 72 ch-3 sps and 12 ch-4 sps.

Rnd 14: Sl st in next dc and in ch-sp of next shell, work beg shell in same ch-sp; *ch 4, sc in next ch-3 sp, (ch 3, sc in next ch-3 sp) 11 times, ch 4, shell in ch-sp of next shell**, shell in ch-sp of next shell; rep from * around, ending last rep at **; join: 12 shells, 66 ch-3 sps and 12 ch-4 sps.

First Pineapple Point

Row 1: Sl st in next dc and in ch-sp of next shell, work beg shell in same ch-sp, ch 4, sc in next ch-3 sp, (ch 3, sc in next ch-3 sp) 10 times, ch 4, shell in ch-sp of next shell: 2 shells and 10 ch-3 sps; ch 5, turn.

Row 2: Shell in ch-sp of first shell, ch 4, sc in next ch-3 sp, (ch 3, sc in next ch-3 sp) 9 times, ch 4, shell in ch-sp of next shell: 2 shells and 9 ch-3 sps; ch 5, turn.

Rows 3 through 10: Rep Row 2, 8 more times, working 1 less (ch 3, sc in next ch-3 sp) in each row than in previous row. At end of Row 10: 2 shells and 1 ch-3 sp; ch 5, turn.

Row 11: Shell in ch-sp of first shell, ch 4, sc in next ch-3 sp, ch 4, 2 dc in ch-sp of next shell, ch 1, do not turn, sl st from front to back in ch-sp of first shell made, ch 1, 2 dc in same ch-sp as last 2 dc made; ch 5, turn; sl st around 2 ch-1 sps. Finish off; weave in ends.

SECOND PINEAPPLE POINT

Row 1: With right side facing, join with sl st in ch-sp of next unworked shell on Rnd 14, work beg shell in same ch-sp, ch 4, sc in next ch-3 sp, (ch 3, sc in next ch-3 sp) 10 times, ch 4, shell in ch-sp of next shell: 2 shells and 10 ch-3 sps; ch 5, turn.

Rows 2 through 11: Work same as Rows 2 through 11 on First Pineapple Point.

THIRD THROUGH SIXTH PINEAPPLE POINTS

Work same as Second Pineapple Point.

FINISHING

Wash and block.

General Instructions

Crochet patterns are written in a special shorthand which is used so that instructions don't take up too much space. They sometimes seem confusing, but once you learn them, you'll have no trouble following them.

Here are some standard abbreviations

approx	approximately
beg	beginning
bet	between
cm	centimeter
cont	continue
dec	decrease
fig	figure
g	grams
inc	increase(ing)
lp(s)	loop(s)
mm	millimeter
oz	ounce(s)
patt	pattern
prev	previous
rem	remain(ing)
rep	repeat(ing)
rnd(s)	round(s)
RS	right side
sk	skip
sl	slip
sp(s)	space(s)
st(s)	stitch(es)
tog	together
WS	wrong side
yd(s)	yard
YO	yarn over hook

These are the standard symbols

*An asterisk (or double asterisks**) in a pattern row indicates a portion of instructions to be used more than once. For instance, "rep from * three times" means that after working the instructions once, you must work them again three times for a total of 4 times in all.

† A dagger (or double daggers ††) indicates that those instructions will be repeated again later in the same row or round.

: The number of stitches after a colon tells you the number of stitches you will have when you have completed the row or round.

( ) Parentheses enclose instructions which are to be worked the number of times following the parentheses. For instance, "(ch 1, sc, ch 1) 3 times" means that you will chain one, work one single crochet, and then chain one again, three times for a total of six chains and three single crochets.

Parentheses often set off or clarify a group of stitches to be worked into the same space or stitch. For instance, "(dc, ch 2, dc) in corner space."

[ ] Brackets and ( ) parentheses are also used to give you additional information. For instance, "(rem sts are left unworked)."

These are standard terms

Finish off—This means to end your piece by pulling the yarn through the last loop remaining on the hook. This will prevent the work from unraveling.

Continue in Pattern (Patt) as Established—This means to follow the pattern stitch as it has been set up, working any increases or decreases in such a way that the pattern remains the same as it was established.

Work even—This means that the work is continued in the pattern as established without increasing or decreasing.

Right Side—This means the side of the garment that will be seen.

Wrong Side—This means the side of the garment that is inside when the garment is worn.

Right Front—This means the part of the garment that will be worn on the right side of the body.

Left Front—This means the part of the garment that will be worn on the left side of the body.

CROCHET TERMINOLOGY

The patterns in this book have been written using the crochet terminology that is used in the United States. Terms which may have different equivalents in other parts of the world are listed below.

UNITED STATES	INTERNATIONAL
Double crochet	treble crochet
Gauge	tension
Half double crochet	half treble crochet
Single crochet	double crochet
Skip	miss
Slip stitch	single crochet
Triple crochet	double treble crochet

FRINGE

Cut yarn to the specified length. Fold the yarn in half. Insert the crochet hook from the front to back of the work. Catch the folded yarn and pull through the crocheted piece, creating a loop. Draw the yarn ends through the loop and pull to tighten them. Trim the yarn pieces to even lengths.